MARK KNOPFLER

BIOGRAPHY

The Musical Journey of a

Guitar Legend From Pub

Gigs to World Tours

Mary J. Harris

Disclaimer

The following book is for informational and educational purposes only. The information presented is without contract or any type of guarantee assurance. While every caution has been taken to provide accurate and current information, it is solely the reader's responsibility to check all information contained in this article before relying upon it. Neither the author nor the publisher can be held accountable for any errors or omissions. Under no circumstances will any legal responsibility or blame be held against the author or publisher for any reparation, damages, or monetary loss due to the information presented, either directly or indirectly. This book is not intended as legal or medical advice. If any such specialized advice is needed, seek a qualified individual for help.

Trademarks are used without permission. Use of the trademark is not authorized by, associated with, or sponsored by the trademark owners. All trademarks and brands used within this book are used with no intent to infringe on the trademark owners and are only used for clarifying purposes.

This book is not sponsored by or affiliated with entertainment, its singers-songwriters, the record producers, the musicians, or anyone involved with them.

Table of Content

INTRODUCTION

Mark Knopfler is a famous figure in the music industry. He is a gifted guitarist and composer whose impact extends well beyond the rock genre. Over the course of several decades, he has made a name for himself as an artist whose creations are adored by people all over the world and receive high praise from critics.

His musical career started modestly, but his skill and commitment soon made him stand out from the crowd. He plays the guitar in a way that is instantly recognizable and has come to define most of his work. His fingerpicking style combines blues, folk, and rock. His distinctive approach and rich, rich voice have mesmerized listeners and cemented his status as one of the greatest artists in the annals of contemporary music.

His position as the main singer, guitarist, and major songwriter of Dire Straits—a band that soon became well-known for its eminently listenable sound—fueled his ascent to fame. Dire Straits saw tremendous commercial success under Knopfler's direction, with albums like *Brothers in Arms* and *Love Over Gold* reaching listeners all over the world. These albums are more than just a list of songs; they are auditory journeys that draw the listener into the narratives and emotional states that Knopfler painstakingly creates. The everlasting quality of his work is attributed to his vivid storytelling and powerful imagery in his music.

In addition to his achievements with Dire Straits, Knopfler has had an equally successful solo career. He has expanded his creative horizons with his solo recordings, fusing blues, folk, and country music with the richness of his lyrics and skill as an instrumentalist that has always characterized his work. He offers audiences fresh perspectives on his craft with every endeavor, showcasing a different aspect of his ingenuity.

His influence on music extends beyond the tracks on his albums. In addition, he has produced, collaborated, and composed with great success. His collaborations with musicians like Tina Turner and Bob Dylan show off his flexibility and the regard he has for the business. His ventures into cinema scoring have also produced noteworthy soundtracks, which have expanded his already varied body of work.

Even with his popularity, Knopfler is a modest and reflective musician who is more concerned with the art of creating music than with the perks of celebrity. His interviews show a reflective person who is devoted to his work and always looking to improve the tone of his voice. His legacy will live on because of the devoted following and critical accolades he has garnered from his work.

His work serves as a constant reminder of the value of authenticity, skill, and narrative in a society where music frequently tends toward the transient. As he keeps touring and recording, he interacts with his fans in a manner that very few musicians of his caliber can, making every show and album release a memorable event. Generations of artists have looked to him for inspiration, demonstrating his impact, and his body of work continues to set the standard for quality in the music business. He has made significant contributions to music as a musician, composer, and artist, and his career is far from over.

CHAPTER 1: EARLY LIFE AND MUSICAL INFLUENCES

Born in Glasgow, Scotland, on August 12, 1949, Mark Knopfler grew up to become one of the most respected guitarists and composers of his time. A wide range of cultural influences shaped his early existence and eventually shaped his musical style. Despite his Glasgow birthplace, at the age of seven, his family relocated to Newcastle upon Tyne, England. His transition from Glasgow's energetic metropolis to Newcastle's more industrial environs would have a significant impact on how he developed as a musician and how he saw the world.

He was exposed to a wide variety of music during his upbringing, encompassing several genres and customs. His mother, Louisa Mary, was an English teacher, and his father, Erwin Knopfler, was an architect and Marxist who had left Hungary to escape the Nazis. Knopfler's family's combination of creative expression and academic discipline fostered a rich atmosphere for his developing creativity. Even though they were not musicians, Mark's parents supported him and his younger brother David in following their passions in the arts.

His family's record collection and the radio shows they tuned in shaped his early musical experiences. He became especially fond of the American South's sounds, which at the time were becoming more and more well-liked in Britain. He was enthralled with the blues because of its profound emotional resonance; he was also drawn to the early rock & roll songs of Chuck Berry, Buddy Holly, and Elvis Presley. These musicians touched a deep chord with young Mark with their unadulterated energy and honest songs. The folk music renaissance that was taking across Britain also drew him in, especially Bob Dylan's songs, whose lyrical depth and straightforward yet potent melodies had a profound effect on him.

Knopfler started experimenting with the guitar at the age of 15, and it would be his constant companion from then on. Mark had a lot of early musical instruction from his part-time musician uncle, Kingsley. It was from

Kingsley's antique guitar that Mark picked up his first chords. With the guitar, Mark was able to express himself and connect with the music he liked, and it soon became an integral part of his life.

He was like a sponge during his adolescence, soaking up all the musical influences around him. He listened to albums for endless hours, attempting to mimic the sounds of his musical idols. During this time, his playing started to take shape, greatly influenced by the fingerpicking methods used by blues and folk guitarists. Instead of using a pick like many of his contemporaries, Knopfler perfected a fingerstyle method that would eventually become his hallmark sound. He was able to produce complex rhythms and melodies at the same time using this method, which gave his music a unique texture that distinguished him from other guitarists.

His quest for learning was as great as his passion for music. He loved to read and was very interested in literature, especially the writings of authors like Cormac McCarthy and Ernest Hemingway. Later on, his songs would show signs of this literary influence, with their dense, narrative-driven lyrics. Knopfler had an increasing passion for music, but he also had a strong intellectual background. He was well-known for his keen intelligence and wit while attending Gosforth Grammar School, where he excelled in the English language.

His musical path took a dramatic shift in his late teens when he picked up an electric guitar. The enhanced audio presented him with novel opportunities, enabling him to experiment with various tones and textures. Jimi Hendrix, whose creative use of the electric guitar stretched the limits of what the instrument could achieve, had a particularly big effect on him. But despite his forays into the electric guitar, Knopfler never gave up on the fingerstyle approach he had honed, which would eventually come to define his playing.

In 1967, Knopfler enrolled at Essex's Harlow College to study journalism after graduating from high school. He continued to immerse himself in music throughout this time, perfecting his technique and performing in several local bands. His work as a journalist helped him hone his storytelling abilities, which later come to be recognized as a signature aspect of his songs. Knopfler continued to be dedicated to his studies even as his interest in music grew, and he eventually graduated from the University of Leeds with a degree in English.

For Knopfler, the years he spent in college were crucial to his career and personal life. In addition to writing his songs, he kept playing in bands and giving performances in neighborhood bars and clubs. His work was quite personal and frequently reflected his life and surroundings. Even though they were unpolished, these early songs had a depth and maturity that would eventually come to define his career.

He was also impacted by the British blues revival at this time, which was spearheaded by groups like Cream and The Rolling Stones. He was impressed by how these musicians had transformed the blues, a style deeply ingrained in African American culture, into their own. Knopfler, nevertheless, wasn't satisfied with just copying these musicians. His goal was to discover his unique style and produce music that reflected his personal experiences and emotions.

During these years, his brother David—who shared his enthusiasm for music—had a significant effect as well. The seeds of what would eventually become Dire Straits were sown during the frequent playdates between the two brothers. But before the band became a reality, a few more years would pass.

He kept honing his guitar and songwriting abilities throughout the meanwhile. He was a very serious musician who was always honing his craft and broadening his musical interests. Although he enjoyed more intricate genres like jazz and classical music, he was drawn to the directness and simplicity of roots music. His work with Dire Straits, where he skillfully combined elements of rock, blues, and folk to create a sound that was all his own, would eventually reflect this broad combination of inspirations.

For Knopfler, the early 1970s were a time of experimentation and discovery. Although he was an English instructor at Loughton College, his real interest was still music. During this period, he participated in several bands, one of which was a pub rock group named Brewers Droop, where he performed live and learned a lot. He also started to establish the lyrical approach that would eventually characterize his work with Dire Straits during this time. His songs frequently have a narrative quality to them, based on his personal experiences and perceptions of the world.

His varied background and exposure to a broad variety of musical genres served as the basis for his success as a musician and songwriter in the future. He had already established a unique sound by the time he joined Dire Straits in 1977, which would help him stand out from the crowd. He would go on to become one of the most renowned characters in rock music thanks to his ability to meld many musical influences into a seamless whole and his astute lyrics.

CHAPTER 2: FORMING DIRE STRAITS

Forming Dire Straits was not just a moment in time but a pivotal chapter in the annals of rock history, driven largely by the musical genius and determination of Mark Knopfler. In the late 1970s, the world of music was in a state of flux, with punk rock crashing through the airwaves, and disco dominating dance floors. It was within this dynamic and rapidly shifting environment that Knopfler, with his unique perspective on music, saw an opportunity to create something that would stand apart from the trends of the day.

At this time, he was honing his craft, playing in various bands, and trying to carve out a niche for himself in the music scene. His influences were eclectic, drawing from folk, blues, country, and rock. This broad spectrum of inspiration allowed him to develop a distinctive guitar style that would later become the hallmark of Dire Straits. His finger-picking technique, combined with his ability to convey emotion through every note, set him apart from his contemporaries.

But forming a band was not simply about showcasing his guitar skills; it was about creating a sound that resonated with an audience that was yearning for something authentic. His vision for Dire Straits was clear from the outset. He wanted to create music that told stories—tales of ordinary people, their struggles, their triumphs, and the world around them. This narrative-driven approach to songwriting would become one of the defining features of the band's music.

In 1977, Mark Knopfler joined forces with his brother, David Knopfler, a rhythm guitarist, and two other musicians—John Illsley on bass and Pick Withers on drums. This quartet would become the founding members of Dire Straits. The name of the band itself was a reflection of their situation at the time. They were in a "dire strait," struggling financially, with little more than their instruments and a dream. But his belief in the music they were creating was strong. He knew they were on the cusp of something significant.

Their early days as a band were marked by hard work and perseverance. The music industry was notoriously tough to break into, especially for a group that did not conform to the prevailing trends. Knopfler, however, was not interested in chasing after fleeting fads. Instead, he focused on perfecting their sound, ensuring that every song they played was a true representation of their artistic intent. This dedication to authenticity would eventually pay off.

The turning point for Dire Straits came with the recording of their demo tape, which included the now-legendary track "Sultans of Swing." This song, with its crisp guitar lines, compelling lyrics, and infectious rhythm, caught the attention of Charlie Gillett, a DJ on BBC Radio London. Gillett's decision to play "Sultans of Swing" on his radio show was a breakthrough moment for the band. The track quickly gained traction, and the band started to build a following.

The success of "Sultans of Swing" was not just a stroke of luck; it was the result of his meticulous craftsmanship as a songwriter and guitarist. The song captured the essence of Dire Straits—simple yet sophisticated, with lyrics that painted vivid pictures of the scenes and characters Knopfler so skillfully described. The public's response to the track was overwhelming, and it wasn't long before Dire Straits found themselves signing a record deal with Phonogram Records.

With their first album on the way, the band was on the brink of something great. The self-titled debut album, "Dire Straits," was released in 1978 and was an immediate success. The album featured a stripped-down, no-frills sound that was a breath of fresh air amidst the excesses of the music scene at the time. It was clear that Knopfler and his bandmates had tapped into something special, something that resonated with listeners across the globe. The success of the album was a testament to the power of Knopfler's vision and the band's ability to execute it flawlessly.

But the road to success was not without its challenges. As the band began to gain fame, the pressures of the music industry started to mount. Touring, recording, and the constant demand for new material put a strain on the members. Knopfler, as the driving force behind the band, bore the brunt of these pressures. His perfectionism, which had been a strength in crafting their unique sound, became a source of tension within the band. The desire to maintain the integrity of their music while navigating the commercial aspects of the industry was a delicate balance.

Despite these challenges, Dire Straits continued to evolve, and their sound matured with each subsequent album. His songwriting became more intricate, and his guitar work more refined. The band's second album, "Communiqué," released in 1979, built on the success of their debut and solidified their place in the rock music scene. The album's success was another validation of Knopfler's talent as a songwriter and a leader.

As the years went on, Dire Straits would go on to release several more albums, each contributing to their legacy as one of the most influential rock bands of their time. Knopfler's ability to craft songs that were both musically complex and lyrically rich set them apart from their peers. His storytelling, combined with the band's musicianship, created a sound that was both timeless and contemporary.

The formation of Dire Straits was not just about creating a band; it was about establishing a musical identity that would endure for decades. His vision and determination were the driving forces behind this success. He was not content to simply follow the trends of the time; he wanted to create something that would last, something that would speak to people on a deeper level. And he did just that.

Dire Straits became more than just a band; they became a symbol of what could be achieved when talent, hard work, and a clear vision come together. His leadership and his ability to bring out the best in his bandmates were key factors in their success. He understood that while he was the primary creative force behind the band, it was the collective effort of all the members that made Dire Straits what it was.

Looking back, it's clear that the formation of Dire Straits was a turning point in rock history. The band's music continues to resonate with audiences today, a testament to the enduring appeal of Knopfler's songwriting and guitar work. His ability to blend different musical styles into something uniquely his own is what set Dire Straits apart and what continues to make their music relevant.

Her journey with Dire Straits is a story of perseverance, creativity, and the pursuit of excellence. It is a story that continues to inspire musicians and fans alike. The formation of Dire Straits was not just the beginning of a band; it was the beginning of a musical legacy that would stand the test of time. His influence on the world of music is undeniable, and the impact of Dire Straits is still felt today, decades after they first burst onto the scene. This is the legacy of him and the band he formed—a legacy that will continue to inspire and influence for generations to come.

CHAPTER 3: RISE TO FAME WITH "SULTANS OF SWING"

Mark Knopfler's rise to fame with "Sultans of Swing" is a story of musical discovery and the perfect timing of creativity meeting opportunity. In the late 1970s, the music scene was brimming with punk rock energy and the airwaves were dominated by fast-paced, rebellious sounds. It was a time when bands were expected to fit a particular mold, echoing the angst and aggression that characterized much of the popular music of that era. However, he, with his band Dire Straits, took a different path. Instead of following the crowd, they brought something refreshingly different, a sound that was more subdued yet deeply compelling, marked by Knopfler's signature fingerpicking guitar style and a narrative lyrical approach that set them apart.

"Sultans of Swing" was born out of a chance experience. Knopfler had been to a pub in South London, where he witnessed a struggling jazz band playing in a nearly empty room. The band, though seemingly resigned to their fate, played on with a quiet dignity. This scene struck a chord with Knopfler, who saw in it the paradox of musicians who, despite their lack of recognition, were dedicated to their craft. The song emerged from this observation, telling the story of a band playing their hearts out for a small, disinterested audience, yet being content with their music and the simple joy it brought them.

When Knopfler penned "Sultans of Swing," it was initially just another song he was working on. He recorded a demo of it in 1977, but the track didn't immediately spark any major interest. It wasn't until Dire Straits recorded it professionally that it began to gain attention. The song's effortless blend of rock and jazz, paired with his distinctive guitar work and conversational vocal delivery, made it stand out from the prevailing music trends of the time.

What made "Sultans of Swing" particularly special was how it captured the essence of a live performance in a way that felt both intimate and expansive. His guitar playing was central to this, his fingers dancing across the strings with a fluidity and precision that seemed almost effortless. The clean, unadorned sound of his Fender Stratocaster, coupled with the clarity of the production, allowed every note to be heard with crystal clarity, drawing listeners into the story he was telling.

The song didn't just break from the high-energy punk and rock that dominated the charts—it reintroduced a more sophisticated form of storytelling in music, one that relied on the strength of the narrative and the musicianship rather than on volume or speed. The lyrics of "Sultans of Swing" are conversational, almost like an observer recounting a vivid memory. Knopfler's vocal delivery is calm, almost detached, yet it carries a weight that draws the listener into the world he's describing.

As "Sultans of Swing" began to receive radio play, it quickly caught the ear of both the public and the industry. It wasn't long before the song started climbing the charts, first in the UK and then internationally. This success was not just a matter of good timing; it was proof of the song's quality and the way it resonated with a wide audience. In an era when music was becoming increasingly polarized, with distinct lines being drawn between genres, "Sultans of Swing" managed to transcend those boundaries. It appealed to rock enthusiasts, jazz aficionados, and even those who were simply fans of great storytelling.

The song's rise on the charts was meteoric, and with it, Dire Straits found themselves thrust into the spotlight. For Knopfler, this newfound fame was a double-edged sword. On one hand, "Sultans of Swing" brought the band recognition and respect, opening doors that had previously been closed. On the other, it placed a spotlight on them that would forever shape the trajectory of their careers. Knopfler, who had previously enjoyed relative anonymity, was now the face of a band that had captured the imagination of the music world.

The song's impact was far-reaching. It not only established Dire Straits as a force to be reckoned with in the music industry but also set the stage for Knopfler's career as one of the most respected guitarists and songwriters of his generation. The success of "Sultans of Swing" allowed the band to tour extensively, bringing their music to audiences around the world. These tours further cemented their reputation, with Knopfler's live performances of the song becoming legendary for their technical brilliance and emotional depth.

"Sultans of Swing" also marked a turning point in how guitarists were perceived in popular music. At a time when flashy, distorted solos were the norm, his clean, melodic playing was a breath of fresh air. His technique was impeccable, but it was his restraint and attention to detail that truly set him apart. Every note served the song, contributing to the overall narrative rather than overshadowing it. This approach would become a hallmark of Knopfler's style, influencing countless guitarists who sought to emulate his precision and feel.

The success of "Sultans of Swing" was also a reflection of the changing tastes of the listening public. As the song climbed the charts, it became clear that there was an appetite for music that was both technically proficient and emotionally resonant. Dire Straits tapped into this desire, offering something that was both familiar and new, blending elements of rock, jazz, and blues into a sound that was distinctly their own.

The release of Dire Straits' debut album, which featured "Sultans of Swing," solidified the band's position in the music world. The album received critical acclaim, with many reviewers praising Knopfler's songwriting and guitar work. It was a remarkable achievement for a band that had only recently formed, and it set the stage for a career that would see them become one of the most successful acts of the 1980s.

But for him, the success of "Sultans of Swing" was not just about commercial achievement. It was about artistic integrity and staying true to his vision as a musician. He resisted the pressures to conform to industry expectations, choosing instead to follow his path. This determination to remain authentic would define his career, both with Dire Straits and as a solo artist.

As the years went by, "Sultans of Swing" continued to hold a special place in the hearts of fans. It became a song that defined an era, a reminder of a time when music was about more than just entertainment—it was about connection, storytelling, and the shared experience of listening to something that moved you. For Knopfler, the song was a testament to the power of music to transcend the ordinary, to take something as simple as a night in a pub and turn it into something universal.

In concert, "Sultans of Swing" became a highlight of Dire Straits' performances, with audiences eagerly awaiting the moment when Knopfler would launch into the song's iconic riff. It was a song that never grew old, its appeal only deepening with time. Even today, decades after its release, it remains a staple of classic rock radio and a favorite among guitarists who admire his technique and style.

The legacy of "Sultans of Swing" goes beyond the success of a single song. It represents a moment in time when a band and a musician found their voice and shared it with the world. It's a song that captured the imagination of millions, introducing them to their unique talent and the music of Dire Straits. While many years have passed since its release, its influence continues to be felt, inspiring new generations of musicians and reminding listeners of the magic that can happen when creativity and passion come together in perfect harmony.

His journey with "Sultans of Swing" is a testament to his enduring talent and his ability to craft songs that resonate on a deep, emotional level. It's a story of how one song can change everything, taking a band from relative obscurity to international fame, and it's a reminder of the power of music to capture the human experience in a way that words alone never could. Through "Sultans of Swing," he didn't just write a hit song—he created a piece of art that continues to inspire and captivate, proving that sometimes, the most unexpected stories are the ones that stay with us the longest.

CHAPTER 4: SUCCESS AND STRUGGLES WITH DIRE STRAITS

Mark Knopfler's journey to success and the struggles he faced along the way is a tale of persistence, creativity, and the sheer force of will needed to rise above dire circumstances. Known for his distinct guitar playing and evocative storytelling, his path was far from easy. The road was paved with challenges that tested his resolve, yet it was his unrelenting dedication to his craft that propelled him to the heights of musical fame.

His rise to prominence began in the late 1970s when he founded the band Dire Straits with his brother David. The group's initial formation was born out of a shared passion for music, but they lacked the resources and connections that many of their contemporaries enjoyed. In the early days, Dire Straits was nothing more than a band struggling to find its place in the bustling music scene of London. The members lived hand to mouth, scraping together what little money they could to afford rehearsal spaces and recording equipment.

The financial struggles were compounded by the fact that the music industry was in a state of flux. Punk rock was dominating the airwaves, and the polished sound that Dire Straits was developing seemed out of step with the prevailing trends. Record labels were hesitant to invest in a band that didn't fit the mold of the moment, and the band faced rejection after rejection. However, Knopfler's determination never wavered. He continued to hone his skills, both as a guitarist and a songwriter, refusing to compromise on the vision he had for his music.

The breakthrough came when the band's self-titled debut album was released in 1978. The single "Sultans of Swing" caught the attention of audiences and critics alike, and it wasn't long before Dire Straits began to gain traction. However, success didn't immediately translate into financial stability. The band was still working under tight budgets, and their early tours were marred by logistical nightmares and the strain of life on the road. The pressure of keeping the band together, coupled with the uncertainty of whether they could sustain their newfound success, weighed heavily on Knopfler's shoulders.

As Dire Straits began to gain more recognition, the demands on Knopfler increased. The relentless touring schedule took a toll on his physical and mental health, and the pressures of fame began to mount. There was the ever-present challenge of meeting the expectations of both fans and the music industry, while also staying true to his artistic vision. The tension between commercial success and artistic integrity became a central struggle for Knopfler during this period. He was determined not to be swayed by the demands of record labels or the desire for mainstream approval, yet the reality of the industry meant that compromise was sometimes unavoidable.

The success of their subsequent albums, such as "Communiqué" and "Making Movies," solidified Dire Straits' position in the music world, but it also brought new challenges. Knopfler found himself increasingly isolated, both creatively and personally. The pressure to deliver hit after hit was immense and the constant scrutiny from the media only added to the burden. Despite the outward appearance of success, Knopfler often felt trapped by the very thing he had worked so hard to achieve. The struggles of balancing the business side of music with his creative instincts became a recurring theme in his life.

By the time "Brothers in Arms" was released in 1985, Dire Straits had reached the pinnacle of their success. The album was a global phenomenon, with hits like "Money for Nothing" and "Walk of Life" dominating the charts. However, with this massive success came an even greater set of challenges. The pressures of touring, media attention, and the expectations of fans and the industry began to take a significant toll on Knopfler. The intense schedule left little time for personal reflection or creative exploration, and the weight of responsibility for the band's success became increasingly difficult to bear.

His struggles during this time were not just professional but also deeply personal. The demands of fame had strained his relationships, and the constant pressure to perform left him feeling exhausted and disillusioned. There was a growing sense of disconnect between the public persona of Mark Knopfler, the rock star, and the private individual who longed for peace. This internal conflict led to a period of introspection, where Knopfler began to question the direction of his life and career. The success that he had fought so hard to achieve now seemed like a double-edged sword, bringing with it as much pain as it did pleasure.

The relentless pace of life in Dire Straits eventually became unsustainable. He began to withdraw from the limelight, seeking solace in his solo work and other creative pursuits. The decision to step away from the band was not an easy one, but it was necessary for his mental and physical well-being. The years of constant touring and the pressures of maintaining the band's success had taken their toll, and Knopfler needed to reclaim his life on his terms. The move towards a solo career allowed him to explore new musical landscapes and reconnect with the joy of making music without the heavy burden of commercial expectations.

His solo career has been marked by a return to the roots of his musical inspirations. Free from the pressures of the mainstream, he has been able to experiment with different styles and collaborate with a wide range of artists. This period of his life has been one of renewal, where he has been able to find a balance between his love of music and his need for personal space. The struggles of his earlier years have given way to a quieter, more reflective phase in his life, where he can create on his terms without the constant pressure of the public eye.

Despite the challenges he faced, his success with Dire Straits remains a defining chapter in his life. The band's music continues to resonate with audiences around the world, a testament to his talent as a songwriter and musician. The struggles he endured along the way have only deepened his appreciation for the simple pleasures of life and the importance of staying true to one's artistic vision. Knopfler's story is not just one of success, but also resilience and the ability to overcome the challenges that life inevitably throws in one's path.

In the years since Dire Straits, he has continued to make music that speaks to the heart, drawing on the rich experiences of his life. His solo work reflects the wisdom and perspective that come with age, offering listeners a glimpse into the mind of an artist who has seen it all but remains deeply connected to the craft that has defined his life. Knopfler's journey has been anything but easy, but it is this very struggle that has shaped him into the musician and person he is today. His story is a reminder that success is not just about achieving fame and fortune, but also about navigating the ups and downs with grace and integrity.

The struggles and successes of his life are proof of the enduring power of passion and perseverance. Through all the challenges, he has remained steadfast in his commitment to his music, never allowing the pressures of fame to dictate his creative choices. His journey is a powerful example of how the trials we face can ultimately lead to a deeper understanding of ourselves and our true calling. His music, rich with the experiences of his life, continues to inspire and resonate with those who listen, a lasting legacy of a man who never gave up on his dreams, no matter how difficult the road became.

CHAPTER 5: SOLO CAREER AND EXPERIMENTATION

Mark Knopfler's solo career is a testament to his relentless pursuit of artistic exploration and a deep commitment to refining his craft as a musician. After achieving monumental success as the frontman and driving force behind Dire Straits, he embarked on a solo journey that allowed him to go into a wide array of musical styles and influences, unbound by the expectations that come with leading a world-renowned band. His solo work showcases a vast range of musical expressions, underpinned by his signature guitar style, nuanced songwriting, and a passion for storytelling.

His transition into a solo career marked a significant shift in his creative approach. Freed from the collaborative nature and commercial pressures of a band, he began to experiment with different genres and sounds, drawing inspiration from folk, blues, country, and even Celtic music. His ability to seamlessly blend these influences into his work highlighted his versatility as a musician and songwriter. Knopfler's solo albums are often characterized by their rich textures and intricate arrangements, which provide the perfect backdrop for his evocative lyrics and melodic guitar lines.

His first solo album, "Golden Heart," released in 1996, set the tone for what would become a long and prolific solo career. This album was a departure from the arena rock sound that had defined much of Dire Straits' work. Instead, "Golden Heart" embraced a more intimate, roots-oriented approach, with Knopfler exploring themes of love, loss, and memory through a collection of deeply personal songs. The album's title track, along with songs like "Darling Pretty" and "Nobody's Got the Gun," revealed a more introspective side to Knopfler's songwriting, blending folk and country elements with his distinctive guitar work.

His subsequent albums continued to build on this foundation, each one offering a unique perspective on his musical journey. "Sailing to Philadelphia," released in 2000, is often regarded as one of his finest solo efforts. The album is a masterful exploration of American roots music, drawing heavily from blues, folk, and country traditions. The title track, a duet with James Taylor, tells the story of two British surveyors, Charles Mason and Jeremiah Dixon, who were tasked with establishing the boundary between Pennsylvania and Maryland. The song, like much of the album, is rich in historical references and vivid imagery, showcasing Knopfler's skill as a storyteller.

Throughout his solo career, he has displayed a keen interest in history and narrative songwriting. Many of his songs are inspired by historical events, places, and figures, giving his music a sense of depth and authenticity that resonates with listeners. His 2002 album "The Ragpicker's Dream" is a prime example of this approach, with songs like "Why Aye Man" and "Hill Farmer's Blues" offering poignant reflections on working-class life and the human condition. The album's sparse production and acoustic arrangements further emphasize the storytelling aspect of Knopfler's music, allowing the lyrics and melodies to take center stage.

His exploration of different musical styles continued with his 2004 album "Shangri-La." This record is notable for its eclectic mix of influences, ranging from blues and rock to jazz and Americana. The album's title is a reference to the Shangri-La recording studio in Malibu, California, where much of the album was recorded. Tracks like "Boom, Like That," inspired by the story of Ray Kroc and the McDonald's empire, and "Song for Sonny Liston," about the troubled boxer, showcase Knopfler's ability to find compelling narratives in unexpected places. The album also features some of his most intricate guitar work, with Knopfler displaying his trademark fingerstyle playing across a variety of different musical settings.

As his solo career progressed, his music became increasingly reflective and personal. Albums like "Kill to Get Crimson" (2007) and "Get Lucky" (2009) saw him revisiting the themes of his earlier work, but with a greater sense of maturity and introspection. These records are marked by their understated arrangements and delicate melodies, which serve to highlight the emotional depth of Knopfler's songwriting. "Get Lucky," in particular, is a deeply autobiographical album, with songs like "Border Reiver" and "Cleaning My Gun" drawing on Knopfler's own experiences and memories.

In addition to his studio albums, his solo career has also been defined by his work as a film composer. Over the years, he has scored several films, including "Local Hero," "The Princess Bride," and "Wag the Dog." His film work is characterized by its subtlety and nuance, with Knopfler's music often serving to enhance the emotional impact of the visuals rather than overshadowing them. His ability to create evocative soundscapes with minimal instrumentation has made him one of the most sought-after film composers of his generation.

His solo work also includes collaborations with a diverse range of artists, from country legend Chet Atkins to Irish folk band The Chieftains. These collaborations have allowed him to further expand his musical horizons, exploring new genres and approaches while still retaining his unique voice as a songwriter and guitarist. His 1990 album with Chet Atkins, "Neck and Neck," is a standout example of this, blending Knopfler's British sensibilities with Atkins' American country style to create a record that is both technically impressive and deeply enjoyable.

Despite the wide-ranging nature of his solo work, Knopfler has always remained true to his core musical values. His music is marked by its attention to detail, both in terms of the arrangements and the lyrics. Knopfler's songs are often miniatures, carefully crafted stories that reveal themselves more fully with each listen. His guitar playing, too, is characterized by its precision and expressiveness, with each note carefully chosen to serve the song.

In recent years, he has continued to release new music and tour extensively, showing no signs of slowing down. His 2015 album "Tracker" and 2018's "Down the Road Wherever" both received critical acclaim, with reviewers praising Knopfler's continued growth as a songwriter and musician. These albums see Knopfler reflecting on his life and career, with songs that touch on themes of aging, memory, and the passage of time. Yet, despite the reflective nature of much of his recent work, his music remains as vital and engaging as ever, a testament to his enduring passion for his craft.

His solo career is a remarkable journey of artistic exploration and experimentation. From his early work in the mid-1990s to his more recent releases, he has consistently pushed the boundaries of his music, exploring new styles and approaches while staying true to his roots as a songwriter and guitarist. His ability to tell stories through song, combined with his distinctive guitar playing, has made him one of the most respected and influential musicians of his generation.

CHAPTER 6: SOUNDTRACK COMPOSITIONS AND COLLABORATIONS

Mark Knopfler's contributions to the world of soundtrack compositions and collaborations stand out as some of the most remarkable aspects of his musical career. Renowned as the frontman and lead guitarist of Dire Straits, his talent extends far beyond the realms of rock music, demonstrating a unique ability to craft compelling soundtracks that resonate deeply with audiences.

His journey into the world of film scoring began in the early 1980s, a time when he was already well-established as a musician. His distinctive guitar style, characterized by fingerpicking and melodic ingenuity, caught the attention of filmmakers who were eager to bring a fresh, emotionally resonant sound to their projects. His first foray into this new domain came with the soundtrack for the film "Local Hero" in 1983, a critically acclaimed British drama directed by Bill

Forsyth. The music Knopfler composed for "Local Hero" marked a significant departure from his work with Dire Straits, showcasing his ability to create atmospheric, evocative pieces that perfectly complemented the film's mood and setting. The soundtrack's most notable track, "Going Home," became an iconic piece, widely recognized and celebrated even outside the context of the film. The success of "Local Hero" not only solidified Knopfler's reputation as a versatile composer but also opened the door for future opportunities in film scoring.

Following the success of "Local Hero," he continued to explore the world of soundtracks, taking on projects that allowed him to further refine his approach to composition. His next major work came with the soundtrack for "Cal," a 1984 film directed by Pat O'Connor. The film, set in Northern Ireland during the Troubles, required a soundtrack that could underscore the tension and emotional complexity of its narrative. Knopfler's compositions for "Cal" were hauntingly beautiful, filled with a sense of melancholy that mirrored the film's themes of love, loss, and conflict. The music was praised for its subtlety and depth, further establishing Knopfler as a composer capable of conveying powerful emotions through his work.

His ability to create music that enhances the story of a film without overshadowing it became a hallmark of his soundtrack work. In 1987, he was approached to compose the soundtrack for "The Princess Bride," a film directed by Rob Reiner that blended elements of fantasy, adventure, and romance. The music Knopfler created for "The Princess Bride" was whimsical and enchanting, capturing the fairytale essence of the story while also adding a layer of emotional depth. Tracks like "Storybook Love" became synonymous with the film, enhancing its charm and enduring appeal. Knopfler's work on "The Princess Bride" demonstrated his versatility as a composer, showing that he could adapt his style to suit a wide range of genres and narratives.

In addition to his solo work on soundtracks, Knopfler has also engaged in numerous collaborations throughout his career, working with other artists and composers to create memorable music. One such collaboration was with the American singer-songwriter Willy DeVille, for whom Knopfler produced the album "Miracle" in 1987.

The album included the track "Storybook Love," which was featured in "The Princess Bride" and earned an Academy Award nomination for Best Original Song. His production work on "Miracle" highlighted his ability to work collaboratively, bringing out the best in other artists while also leaving his distinctive mark on the music.

His collaborative efforts extend beyond the world of film and into various other musical projects. He has worked with a diverse range of artists across different genres, lending his skills as a guitarist, producer, and composer to projects that have expanded his musical horizons. One notable collaboration was with the American blues musician Chet Atkins, with whom Knopfler recorded the album "Neck and Neck" in 1990. The album was a critical and commercial success, blending Knopfler's distinctive guitar style with Atkins' virtuosity to create a collection of tracks that celebrated the rich traditions of country and blues music. The partnership between Knopfler and Atkins was a meeting of musical minds, resulting in an album that was both technically impressive and deeply enjoyable.

Another significant collaboration in his career was with the legendary American singer-songwriter Bob Dylan. He had previously played guitar on Dylan's album "Slow Train Coming" in 1979, and the two musicians reunited in 1983 for Dylan's album "Infidels," which Knopfler co-produced. The collaboration was a fruitful one, with Knopfler's production adding a polished yet organic sound to Dylan's tracks. The album was well-received, with critics praising the synergy between Dylan's songwriting and his production work. This partnership was further evidence of Knopfler's ability to work effectively with other artists, bringing his unique perspective to their music while also respecting their creative vision.

His soundtrack work continued to evolve in the 1990s and 2000s, as he took on projects that allowed him to explore new musical territories. In 1997, he composed the soundtrack for the film "Wag the Dog," a political satire directed by Barry Levinson. The music for "Wag the Dog" was more experimental in nature, with Knopfler incorporating elements of electronic music and unconventional instrumentation to create a sound that was both innovative and fitting for the film's satirical tone. This project showcased Knopfler's willingness to push the boundaries of his music, experimenting with new sounds and techniques to serve the needs of the film.

In addition to his work on soundtracks, he has also contributed to various compilations and projects that have allowed him to collaborate with a wide range of artists. One such project was the album "Sailing to Philadelphia" in 2000, which featured a diverse array of guest artists, including James Taylor and Van Morrison. The album was a concept record based on Thomas Pynchon's novel "Mason & Dixon," and Knopfler's compositions reflected the historical and geographical themes of the book. The collaborations on "Sailing to Philadelphia" demonstrated Knopfler's ability to create music that is both thematically rich and musically diverse, drawing on a wide range of influences to create a cohesive and engaging album.

Throughout his career, his approach to soundtrack composition and collaboration has been characterized by a deep respect for the power of music to enhance storytelling. Whether working on a film score, producing an album, or collaborating with other artists, Knopfler has consistently demonstrated an ability to create music that resonates on an emotional level, elevating the projects he is involved in. His work has been recognized with numerous awards and accolades, but perhaps the greatest testament to his skill as a composer and collaborator is the enduring impact his music has had on audiences around the world.

In recent years, he has continued to explore new avenues for his music, taking on projects that challenge him to push the boundaries of his creativity. His work remains as vital and relevant as ever, a testament to his enduring talent and dedication to his craft. Through his soundtracks and collaborations, he has left an indelible mark on the world of music, creating a legacy that will continue to inspire and influence future generations of musicians and composers.

CHAPTER 7: LATER YEARS WITH DIRE STRAITS

Mark Knopfler's later years with Dire Straits were a time marked by both immense success and internal challenges, shaping the final chapters of the band's history. As the frontman and creative force behind Dire Straits, his unique guitar playing, songwriting abilities, and understated vocal style continued to define the band's sound, which by the 1980s had become a cornerstone of rock music.

By the time Dire Straits entered its later years, the band had already achieved global stardom. However, with success came an increasing level of pressure and expectations. Knopfler, known for his meticulous attention to detail, found himself navigating the demands of a massive audience while still striving to remain true to his artistic vision. This period saw the band embracing a more polished and expansive sound, a direction that would both cement their place in music history and lead to significant tensions within the group.

In 1985, Dire Straits released "Brothers in Arms," an album that would become one of the best-selling albums worldwide. It was a milestone in their career, propelled by the success of singles such as "Money for Nothing," "Walk of Life," and the title track "Brothers in Arms." The album's production was marked by an embrace of digital technology, which gave it a crisp, modern sound that resonated with the zeitgeist of the mid-1980s. The iconic guitar riff of "Money for Nothing," accompanied by its groundbreaking music video, became an anthem of the MTV generation, cementing Knopfler's status as one of rock's most innovative guitarists.

However, the success of "Brothers in Arms" also brought new challenges. The grueling tour that followed the album's release took a toll on the band members, both physically and emotionally. The tour was massive, spanning several continents, and featured state-of-the-art production that set a new standard for live performances. Yet, the relentless pace and the scale of the operation began to strain the relationships within the band. Knopfler, who had always preferred a more intimate and controlled environment, found the pressures of such a large-scale production to be overwhelming. His desire to maintain artistic integrity while navigating the commercial demands of the music industry created a significant amount of stress.

As the tour continued, the band's internal dynamics began to shift. Knopfler's role as the leader became more pronounced, and while his vision had driven Dire Straits to great heights, it also led to increasing isolation. The other members of the band, who had initially shared a sense of camaraderie and mutual respect, began to feel the weight of Knopfler's perfectionism. This tension was further exacerbated by the grueling schedule, which left little room for rest or creative recharge.

The years following "Brothers in Arms" were marked by a sense of uncertainty. Knopfler, while still deeply committed to his music, began to explore other creative avenues. His interest in film scoring had been growing, and during this time, he composed music for several films, including "The Princess Bride" and "Local Hero." These projects allowed Knopfler to experiment with different musical styles and provided a welcome break from the demands of leading a globally successful rock band.

By the late 1980s, Dire Straits was at a crossroads. Knopfler, who had always been the driving force behind the band, was increasingly drawn to his solo work and collaborations with other artists. This period of creative exploration was a double-edged sword; while it allowed Knopfler to expand his musical horizons, it also signaled the beginning of the end for Dire Straits. The band released "On Every Street" in 1991, six years after "Brothers in Arms." The album, while successful, did not achieve the same level of critical or commercial acclaim as its predecessor. Nevertheless, it contained several standout tracks, including "Calling Elvis," "Heavy Fuel," and "The Bug," which showcased his continued prowess as a songwriter and guitarist.

The tour that followed "On Every Street" was another massive undertaking, but it was clear that the magic that had once defined Dire Straits was beginning to fade. The tour, which lasted over a year, was one of the band's most ambitious, but it also took a significant toll on Knopfler and the other members. The long stretches on the road, coupled with the pressures of meeting fan expectations and the demands of performing night after night, left Knopfler feeling increasingly disillusioned.

By the time the tour ended in 1992, he had decided to disband Dire Straits. The band had achieved more than he had ever imagined, but the cost had been high. Knopfler was exhausted, both physically and mentally, and the joy that had once driven his creative process was overshadowed by the relentless demands of maintaining the band's success. He was ready to move on, to pursue new projects that allowed him the freedom to explore music on his terms.

After the dissolution of Dire Straits, Knopfler focused on his solo career, releasing a series of critically acclaimed albums that showcased his continued evolution as a musician. These solo projects, while less commercially oriented than his work with Dire Straits, allowed Knopfler to reconnect with the aspects of music that he had always loved: storytelling, intricate guitar work, and a deep connection to his roots in folk, blues, and country music.

In the years following the end of Dire Straits, his legacy as a musician and songwriter only grew. He continued to be celebrated for his contributions to music, both as the leader of one of the most successful rock bands of all time and as a solo artist who refused to be confined by the expectations of the industry. While Dire Straits remains an indelible part of Knopfler's career, his later years with the band were marked by a sense of closure. He had taken Dire Straits to the pinnacle of success, but in doing so, he had also come to realize the importance of following his path.

While the band's final chapter may have been tinged with challenges and internal struggles, it also solidified Knopfler's reputation as one of the most talented and respected musicians of his generation. His ability to balance commercial success with a deep commitment to his craft remains a defining characteristic of his career, both during his time with Dire Straits and beyond.

CHAPTER 8: LEGACY AND IMPACT ON THE MUSIC INDUSTRY

Mark Knopfler's legacy in the music industry is monumental, marked by his unique ability to blend genres and create a sound that is unmistakably his own. From the moment his fingers first danced across a guitar, he carved out a place in music history, not just as a guitarist but as a composer, songwriter, and producer whose influence stretches across decades and continents. His impact on the music industry is both deep and enduring, resonating in the hearts of fans and fellow musicians alike.

His style on the guitar is what first drew attention. He has always been known for his fingerpicking technique, a method that gives his playing a distinct, fluid sound that sets him apart from his peers. His approach to the guitar is as much about what he doesn't play as what he does. He has an innate understanding of space and timing, knowing when to let the notes breathe and when to let them soar. This restraint and precision are what make his solos not just impressive but deeply emotional. Knopfler's playing is not about showing off technical prowess, although he certainly possesses that in spades; it's about conveying a mood, telling a story, and drawing the listener into the heart of the music.

The formation of Dire Straits in the late 1970s was a turning point, not just for Knopfler, but for rock music as a whole. At a time when punk rock was dominating the airwaves with its raw energy and DIY ethos, Knopfler brought a different sensibility to the table. Dire Straits' sound was clean, precise, and sophisticated, characterized by Knopfler's intricate guitar work and his gravelly, understated vocals. Songs like "Sultans of Swing" showcased his ability to craft lyrics that were as evocative as his guitar lines, painting pictures with words as vividly as with music. This ability to merge storytelling with musicianship became a hallmark of Knopfler's career.

As the driving force behind Dire Straits, Knopfler led the band to global success, with albums like "Brothers in

Arms" becoming some of the best-selling records of all time. But Knopfler's contribution to the music industry goes far beyond the success of his band. He has always been an artist who pushes boundaries, exploring new sounds and ideas while staying true to his musical roots. His solo career, which began in the 1990s, allowed him to delve even deeper into his creative instincts, producing a body of work that is diverse and richly textured. Whether exploring folk, blues, country, or rock, Knopfler has always brought a distinctive voice to his music, one that is instantly recognizable yet constantly growing.

His influence extends well beyond his recordings. As a producer and session musician, he has worked with some of the biggest names in music, including Bob Dylan, Tina Turner, and Eric Clapton. His production work is characterized by meticulous attention to detail and a focus on capturing the essence of a song rather than overwhelming it with unnecessary embellishments. Knopfler's collaborations are often marked by deep mutual respect between artists, with his contributions enhancing the work of others without overshadowing them.

One of the most significant aspects of his legacy is his role in redefining what it means to be a guitar hero. In an era where rock guitarists were often seen as larger-than-life figures, Knopfler stood out for his humility and his focus on the music rather than the persona. He has never been one to chase fame or indulge in the excesses that often come with rock stardom. Instead, he has always remained grounded, letting his music speak for itself. This approach has earned him the admiration not just of fans, but of fellow musicians who see him as a true artist, someone who is in it for the love of the craft rather than the accolades.

His impact on the music industry can also be seen in the countless guitarists who cite him as an influence. His style has been studied, emulated, and revered by musicians across genres, from rock and blues to country and folk. Yet, despite his influence, Knopfler remains a singular figure, someone whose sound is so unique that it can never truly be replicated. He has inspired a generation of guitarists to focus on tone, feel, and emotion rather than speed and flash, reminding them that the most important thing in music is not how fast you can play but how deeply you can connect with the listener.

Throughout his career, Knopfler has shown a remarkable ability to adapt and innovate. He has never been content to rest on his laurels, always seeking new challenges and new ways to express himself. Whether scoring films, writing for other artists, or embarking on ambitious solo projects, Knopfler's creative output has remained consistently high, reflecting his deep passion for music and his relentless pursuit of excellence.

In many ways, Knopfler's legacy is defined by his authenticity. He has never tried to be something he's not, and that honesty has resonated with audiences around the world. His music is deeply rooted in tradition, yet it always feels fresh and relevant, a testament to his ability to draw from the past while looking toward the future. Knopfler's songs often explore themes of love, loss, and the passage of time, yet they do so in a way that is both personal and universal. His lyrics are filled with vivid imagery and keen observations, offering listeners a window into his world while also reflecting on their own experiences.

As the years go by, his influence on the music industry only seems to grow. His work continues to be celebrated by critics and fans alike, and his songs remain as powerful today as they were when they were first released. In an industry that is often driven by trends and fleeting success, Knopfler's music has stood the test of time, a reminder that true artistry is not about following the crowd, but about staying true to oneself.

His legacy is one of quiet revolution. He has changed the way we think about the guitar, about songwriting, and about what it means to be a musician. His impact on the music industry is immeasurable, and his influence will be felt for generations to come. As he continues to create and perform, he remains a beacon of integrity and creativity, a true master of his craft who has left an indelible mark on the world of music.

CHAPTER 9: PERSONAL LIFE AND PHILOSOPHY

Mark Knopfler has always carried a deep sense of introspection and authenticity in his personal life and philosophy. For someone who has achieved monumental success in the music world, he remains an emblem of humility and down-to-earth wisdom, qualities that resonate through his private life and artistic endeavors.

One cannot explore his personal life without acknowledging the quietness with which he has lived it. Despite the limelight that follows him, he has always preferred the shadows, the quiet moments that allow for reflection and creation. He is a man who values privacy, and this preference has shaped the way he interacts with the world. Knopfler's personal life is not one of scandal or spectacle; rather, it is marked by a deliberate and careful choice to stay grounded, even when fame could have easily carried him away.

His philosophy, much like his music, is rooted in authenticity. He believes in the importance of staying true to oneself, a principle that has guided him through decades of both personal and professional challenges. His approach to life is one of simplicity, rejecting the trappings of excess that often come with success. Instead, he finds fulfillment in the smaller, more intimate aspects of life—family, friendship, and the quiet satisfaction of a job well done. This philosophy extends to his music, where the honesty of his lyrics and the clarity of his guitar work speak to his belief in the power of simplicity and sincerity.

Family plays a significant role in his personal life. He is a devoted husband and father, and these roles have brought him immense joy and a sense of purpose. Despite his demanding career, Knopfler has always made time for his family, understanding that success in the public eye means little if one's relationships are neglected. He speaks often of the grounding effect his family has had on him, keeping him connected to the real world amidst the surreal experiences of fame. This family connection is not just a source of personal contentment for Knopfler, but also a key element of his philosophy on life—one where love, loyalty, and close relationships are valued above all else.

His philosophy also finds expression in his deep appreciation for history and tradition. He is a man who respects the past and understands the lessons it holds. This reverence for history is evident in both his music and his outlook. Knopfler often speaks of the importance of understanding where one comes from, both in a cultural and a personal sense. This understanding has helped him navigate the complexities of life and fame, offering a steady compass that guides his decisions and actions.

In his personal life, Knopfler is known for his introspective nature. He is not one to seek out the limelight, and this introspection allows him to maintain a balanced perspective on his success. He is a thinker, someone who considers his actions carefully and who finds solace in moments of solitude. This reflective nature is an integral part of his personality, influencing everything from his music to his relationships. It is this introspection that has allowed Knopfler to remain grounded, even when the world around him seemed to be spiraling into chaos.

His love for music is, of course, a central part of his life, but it is also a reflection of his philosophy. For him, music is not just a career or a means to fame—it is a way of life, a language through which he expresses his deepest thoughts and emotions. He has often spoken about the meditative quality of playing the guitar, the way it allows him to lose himself in the moment and connect with something greater than himself. This connection to music is deeply personal for Knopfler, and it is something he approaches with a sense of reverence and respect.

Despite his fame, Mark Knopfler is a man of simple pleasures. He finds joy in the small things—spending time with family, walking in the countryside, and, of course, playing music. These simple pleasures are not just hobbies for Knopfler; they are an essential part of his life philosophy. He believes in the importance of balance, of finding contentment in everyday life rather than constantly chasing after something bigger or better. This approach to life has helped him maintain his sanity and his sense of self in an industry that often pushes people to their limits.

His personal life is also marked by a strong sense of loyalty. He is someone who values long-lasting relationships and who understands the importance of trust and reliability. This loyalty extends to his family, friends, and even his fans. Knopfler is known for his dedication to those close to him, and this dedication is a reflection of his broader philosophy on life—one that values integrity, honesty, and mutual respect.

In conversations about his philosophy, Knopfler often touches on the theme of gratitude. He is acutely aware of how fortunate he has been in his life and career, and this awareness has fostered a deep sense of gratitude in him. Knopfler does not take his success for granted; instead, he sees it as a gift, one that comes with responsibilities. This sense of gratitude is not just something Knopfler feels; it is something he lives by. It influences the way he interacts with others, the way he approaches his work and the way he navigates the challenges of life.

His personal life and philosophy are also influenced by his love of storytelling. He is a natural storyteller, both in his music and in his everyday life. For Knopfler, stories are a way to make sense of the world, to understand the human experience, and to connect with others. This love of storytelling is a central part of his identity, and it is something that has shaped his outlook on life. Knopfler believes in the power of stories to bring people together, to foster empathy, and to inspire change. This belief is not just something he talks about; it is something he embodies in his music and his interactions with others.

Despite the immense success he has achieved, he remains a humble and introspective individual. He is someone who has never let fame change him and who has always remained true to himself and his values. This authenticity is a key part of his philosophy, and it is something that has earned him the respect and admiration of those around him. Knopfler's humility is not just a public persona; it is a genuine reflection of who he is as a person. He understands that success is fleeting and that what really matters are the lasting relationships and the impact one has on others.

In his personal life, he is also known for his generosity. He is someone who gives back, both through his music and through his actions. Whether it's supporting charitable causes or simply being there for a friend in need, Knopfler's generosity is a reflection of his belief in the importance of helping others. This generosity is not just about giving money or resources; it is about giving time, attention, and care to those who need it. For Knopfler, this is not just a duty; it is a way of life.

His philosophy on life is also deeply connected to his understanding of time. He is someone who values the present moment, who understands that life is short and that it is important to make the most of the time we have. This understanding of time has shaped the way Knopfler approaches his life and his work. He is not someone who dwells on the past or worries excessively about the future; instead, he focuses on the here and now, on making the most of each day. This focus on the present is a central part of Knopfler's philosophy, and it is something that has helped him find peace and contentment in his life.

His personal life and philosophy are a reflection of his deep sense of authenticity, humility, and introspection. He is a man who values simplicity, loyalty, and gratitude, and who approaches life with a sense of purpose and balance. His philosophy is not just something he talks about; it is something he lives by, in both his personal life and his music. He is someone who has achieved great success but who has never lost sight of what matters. For Mark Knopfler, life is about more than just fame and fortune—it is about staying true to oneself, valuing the people who matter, and finding joy in the simple, everyday moments. This philosophy has not only shaped his life but has also made him a beloved figure in the world of music and beyond.

CHAPTER 10: ONGOING INFLUENCE AND FUTURE PROJECTS

Mark Knopfler's ongoing influence in the world of music is a testament to his enduring passion, talent, and dedication to his craft. Despite having achieved monumental success with Dire Straits, he continues to push boundaries, exploring new creative avenues and evolving as an artist. His work remains relevant, resonating with both long-time fans and newer generations who discover his music.

In recent years, he has focused on refining his solo career, producing albums that showcase his signature guitar playing, thoughtful lyrics, and deep understanding of various musical genres. His ability to blend rock, folk, blues, and country into a distinctive sound has only matured with time, leading to critically acclaimed albums that reflect his growth as a musician and storyteller. Each album he releases adds another layer to his already impressive body of work, offering fresh perspectives and nuanced compositions that engage listeners on multiple levels.

Beyond recording and performing, he has expanded his influence into other areas of music and entertainment. He has continued to contribute to film soundtracks, a field he has been involved in since the 1980s. His work in this area allows him to explore the intersection of music and visual storytelling, bringing his unique voice to the cinematic experience. His soundtracks, whether for major motion pictures or smaller projects, consistently receive praise for their ability to enhance the emotional depth and narrative arc of the films they accompany.

His collaborations with other artists have also played a significant role in his ongoing influence. He has worked with a wide range of musicians, from well-known figures in the industry to emerging talents, bringing his expertise and creativity to their projects. These collaborations not only highlight his versatility as an artist but also demonstrate his commitment to nurturing and supporting the broader music community. Whether as a producer, session musician, or guest performer, his contributions to these collaborations are always substantial, adding a distinctive quality that elevates the overall work.

As a live performer, he remains as engaging as ever. His tours are events that draw large crowds, eager to experience his music in person. Despite the challenges posed by the global pandemic, Knopfler has found ways to maintain his connection with his audience. He has embraced digital platforms, offering virtual performances and engaging with fans through social media. These efforts have allowed him to continue sharing his music and connecting with people, even when traditional touring was not possible. His adaptability in these times speaks to his understanding of the changing dynamics of the music industry and his willingness to embrace new technologies to reach his audience.

He shows no signs of slowing down. He continues to write and record new music, exploring themes that reflect his current interests and experiences. His approach to songwriting remains deeply personal, drawing from his observations of the world around him and his reflections on life. This introspective quality in his music ensures that his work continues to resonate on a deep level with listeners.

In addition to his solo projects, Knopfler remains open to exploring new collaborations and musical ventures. His curiosity and willingness to experiment have led him to explore genres and styles that may be outside of his traditional comfort zone. This openness to new experiences keeps his music fresh and exciting, both for himself and for his audience. Fans can look forward to hearing how these new influences shape his future work.

His ongoing influence also extends to his role as a mentor and supporter of young artists. He has taken an active interest in the next generation of musicians, offering guidance, support, and opportunities to those just starting. His involvement in this area is driven by a genuine desire to give back to the industry that has given him so much. By sharing his knowledge and experience, Knopfler helps to shape the future of music, ensuring that his legacy will continue to inspire and influence for years to come.

His impact is felt in the way he approaches his craft. He is known for his meticulous attention to detail, whether it is in the studio, on stage, or in the way he handles his guitar. This dedication to excellence serves as a model for other musicians, who look up to him not just for his talent, but for his work ethic and commitment to the art of music. His approach to making music—focusing on quality over quantity, authenticity over trendiness—resonates with artists who seek to create meaningful and lasting work.

His future projects are likely to continue reflecting his broad range of interests and influences. Whether he is working on a new solo album, collaborating with other artists, or composing music for film, his work is certain to be marked by the same creativity and artistry that have defined his career thus far. He remains deeply committed to his music, and his ongoing exploration of new ideas ensures that his future projects will be as innovative and compelling as his past work.

His ongoing influence in the world of music is undeniable. He continues to create, perform, and collaborate at a high level, contributing to the richness and diversity of contemporary music. His work not only honors his artistic legacy but also serves as a guiding light for future generations of musicians. As he moves forward in his career, there is no doubt that he will continue to make significant contributions to the world of music, leaving an indelible mark that will be felt for years to come. His future projects will likely surprise and delight his audience, further cementing his status as one of the most important and influential musicians of our time.

CONCLUSION

Mark Knopfler's legacy as a musician is etched in the annals of rock history. The brilliance of his artistry and the breadth of his influence are undeniable. As a guitarist, songwriter, and producer, he has always approached his craft with a quiet, introspective intensity that belies the enormous impact of his work. His career, spanning decades, is a testament to his dedication to music and his ability to continually evolve and adapt to the changing landscapes of the industry.

The culmination of his career is a reflection of his relentless pursuit of musical excellence and a deep-rooted commitment to authenticity. His journey through the music world has been marked by a unique blend of technical skill and emotional depth, qualities that have set him apart from his peers and endeared him to millions of fans worldwide. Knopfler's music has always been about more than just notes and chords; it is about storytelling, capturing the essence of human experience, and translating that into sound. His ability to convey complex emotions through his guitar playing is unparalleled, and it is this emotional resonance that has made his work timeless.

His contributions to music cannot be overstated. His influence is evident in the countless musicians who cite him as an inspiration and in the enduring popularity of his songs. He has a unique ability to blend different genres and styles, creating a sound that is distinctly his own. Whether it is the bluesy undertones of his guitar work or the folk-inspired narratives of his lyrics, Knopfler's music is always rooted in a deep understanding and appreciation of the traditions that have come before him. Yet, he is never content to merely replicate the past; instead, he pushes boundaries and explores new sonic territories, always seeking to expand his musical horizons.

In the latter stages of his career, he has continued to produce music that is both innovative and reflective. His solo work, in particular, has allowed him to explore new creative avenues, free from the constraints of commercial expectations. These albums, while perhaps not as commercially successful as his work with Dire Straits, have been critically acclaimed and have further solidified his reputation as one of the most important and influential musicians of his generation. Knopfler's willingness to take risks and experiment with new sounds is a testament to his artistic integrity and his refusal to be pigeonholed into a single genre or style.

His live performances are another aspect of his career that deserves recognition. On stage, he is a master of his craft, effortlessly blending technical precision with raw emotion. His concerts are not just about playing the hits; they are about creating an experience for the audience, a journey through the highs and lows of life, told through the medium of music. Knopfler's connection with his audience is palpable, and it is this connection that has made his live shows so memorable. He is a performer who understands the power of music to move people, to bring them together, and to create lasting memories.

The impact of his music goes beyond just the notes he plays or the songs he writes. It is about the way he makes his audience feel, the emotions he evokes, and the stories he tells. His music is a reflection of his own experiences, his observations of the world, and his deep understanding of the human condition. Knopfler's lyrics are often poignant and thought-provoking, dealing with themes of love, loss, and the passage of time. Yet, there is always a sense of hope and resilience in his music, a belief in the enduring power of the human spirit.

As his career draws to a close, it is clear that his influence will be felt for generations to come. He has left an indelible mark on the world of music, and his legacy is one of excellence, innovation, and authenticity. Knopfler's work has transcended the boundaries of genre and time, and his contributions to the art of music will continue to inspire and resonate with people for years to come.

In the end, his career is a testament to the power of music to touch people's lives. He has created a body of work that is both deeply personal and universally relatable, music that speaks to the heart and the soul. Knopfler's legacy is not just in the albums he has released or the awards he has won but in the millions of people who have been moved by his music and who have found comfort, joy, and inspiration in his songs. He is a true artist, one who has dedicated his life to his craft and who has never wavered in his commitment to creating music that is honest, meaningful, and enduring.

As we reflect on his career, it is clear that he has achieved something truly remarkable. He has not only mastered his instrument and honed his craft but has also created a body of work that will stand the test of time. Knopfler's music is a reflection of his journey, his struggles, and his triumphs. It is music that speaks to the human experience in all its difficulty, music that resonates with people on a deep and personal level.

In a world where trends come and go, and where success is often measured in fleeting moments of fame, Mark Knopfler has remained a constant, a beacon of artistic integrity and excellence. He has stayed true to his vision, creating music that is timeless and enduring. Knopfler's legacy is one of creativity, innovation, and passion, and it is a legacy that will continue to inspire and influence for generations to come.

As we conclude our reflection on his career, it is important to acknowledge the profound impact he has had on the world of music. He is not just a musician; he is a storyteller, a poet, and a true artist. His music has the power to move, inspire, and connect people in ways that few other art forms can. Knopfler's legacy is one of passion, dedication, and a relentless pursuit of excellence, and it is a legacy that will continue to resonate with people for many years to come.

In the end, his music is more than just sound; it is a reflection of life itself, with all its beauty, its pain, and its joy. It is music that speaks to the soul, music that has the power to heal, to comfort, and to inspire. His legacy is one of authenticity, creativity, and a deep love for the art of music, and it is a legacy that will continue to inspire and influence for generations to come. His contributions to music are immeasurable, and his impact will be felt long after the final note has been played.

His journey through the world of music is a story of dedication, passion, and an unwavering commitment to his craft. He has created a body of work that is not only musically brilliant but also deeply meaningful and emotionally resonant. His music has the power to touch people's lives, to connect with them on a deep and personal level, and to create lasting memories. As we look back on his career, it is clear that he has achieved something truly remarkable, and his legacy will continue to inspire and resonate with people for many years to come.

Made in United States
Troutdale, OR
12/14/2024

26499565R00046